Printed in Great Britain
by Amazon

Letter Formation for Left-Handed Learners

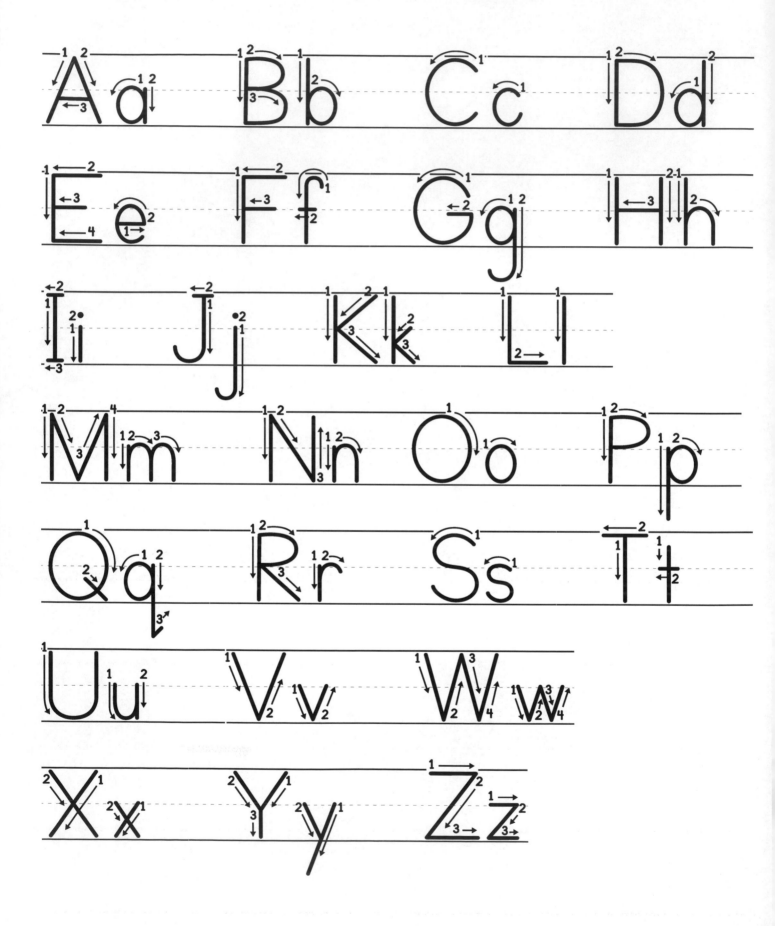

My brother is on a
baseball team.
There are ten kids
on his team. Today
is their big game.

_____

_____

_____

_____

Do you know a male turkey is called a tom and a female turkey is called a hen?

_____

_____

_____

_____

My sister went to a
birthday party on
Sunday. She played
a lot of games at
the party.

_____

_____

_____

_____

We went to
camping in the
mountains. We built
a campfire. Then,
we slept in a tent.

_____

_____

_____

_____

_____

Steven is a good friend. He likes to play piano. He is my neighbor. Steven has two brothers.

_____

_____

_____

_____

It is not raining yet.
It is going to rain in
few hours. We
want to play in the
rain.

We went to the

park during our

spring break. It

was fun!

My cat has beautiful eyes. Her fur is soft. I love to hug her.

I have a pet dog. I
walk him everyday.
I love my dog. He
loves me too.

I went to the
library with my
mom. We
borrowed books.

Don't go outside.
It is snowing very
heavily. The roads
are slippery.

Mary and her brother are riding their bikes in the park.

He is going to

meet his new

teacher at school

today.

I am smart and
kind.

Today is a great
day!

We had a great
time at the party!

I am excited to
go to the library.

I ate a sandwich
for lunch.

Thank you for
inviting us.

Do you mind
singing a song?

She can read
chapter books.

They went fishing
after school.

I got a new pair of
shoes yesterday.

She is walking her

dog.

Everyone is ready

to go out.

I have some
schoolwork to do.

Did you see her
at school today?

She sings well.

They are running.

See! Butterflies.

Are you hungry?

Where is the book?

I see the red car.

We like to write.

He has a coat.

I like my teacher.

Do you like math?

Cat hates water.

It is cold outside.

I play football.

Do you play chess?

She likes apples.

How are you?

Part 3
Sentences

appreciate

friendship

expertize

checkbook

squirrel

morning

birthday

Christmas

about

after

while

below

above

brave

drink

earth

where

which

agent

award

beach

event

begin

faith

sheep

globe

adult

basic

hello

other

since

until

cold

bank

home

help

busy

many

head

hand

bear

feel

back

from

save

near

cook

come

sock

warm

long

stop

fork

gone

baby

arch

laugh

away

under

again

many

their

body

coin

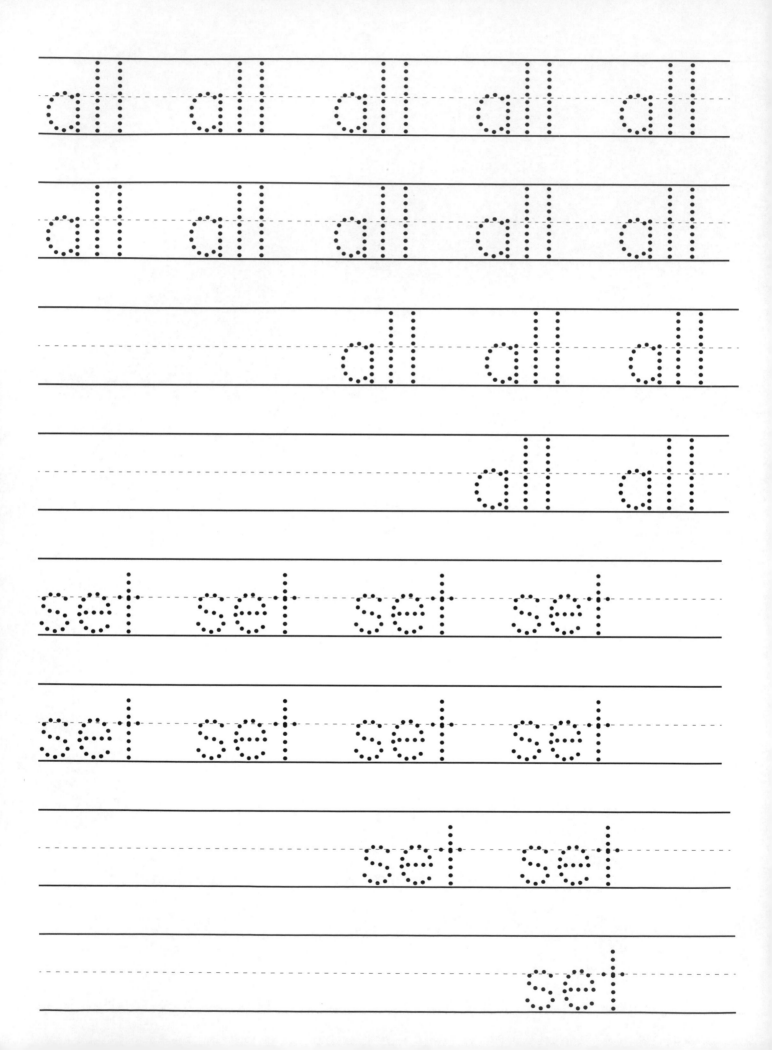

and and and and

and and and and

and and

and

not not not not

not not not not

not not

not

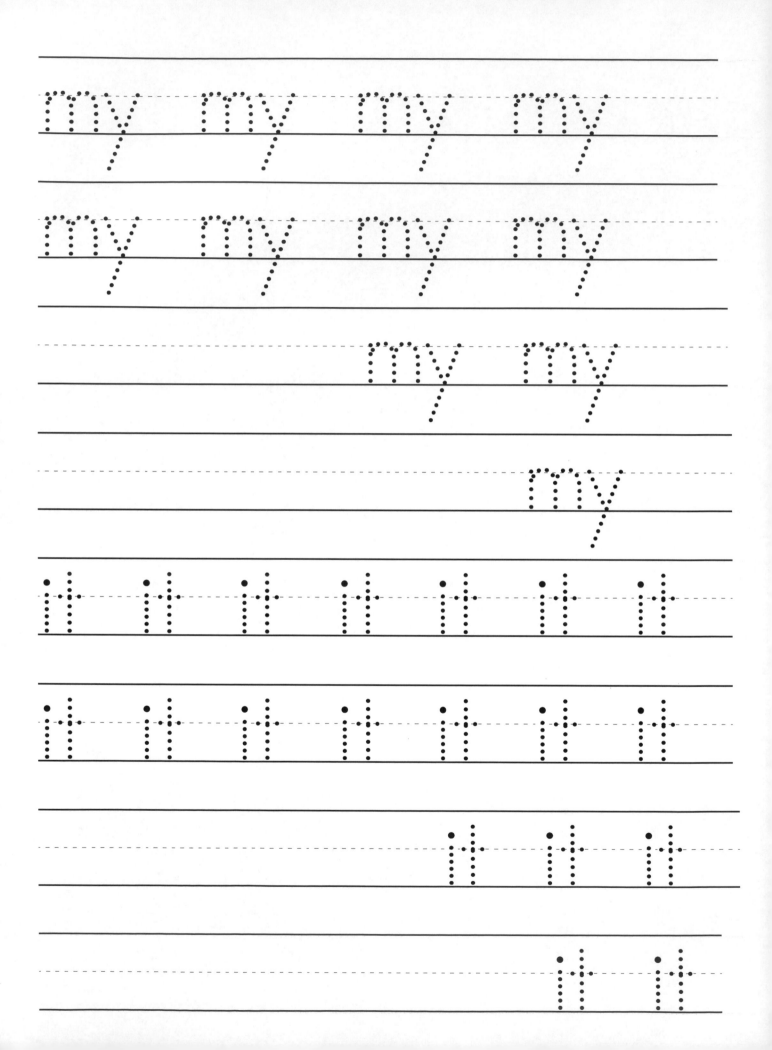

as   as   as   as   as

as   as   as   as   as

as   as

as

of   of   of   of   of

of   of   of   of   of

of   of   of

of   of

up up up up up

up up up up up

up up up

up

be be be be be

be be be be be

be be be

be

is is is is is is is

is is is is is is is

is is is is

is is

we we we we we

we we we we we

we we we

we

Part 2
Words

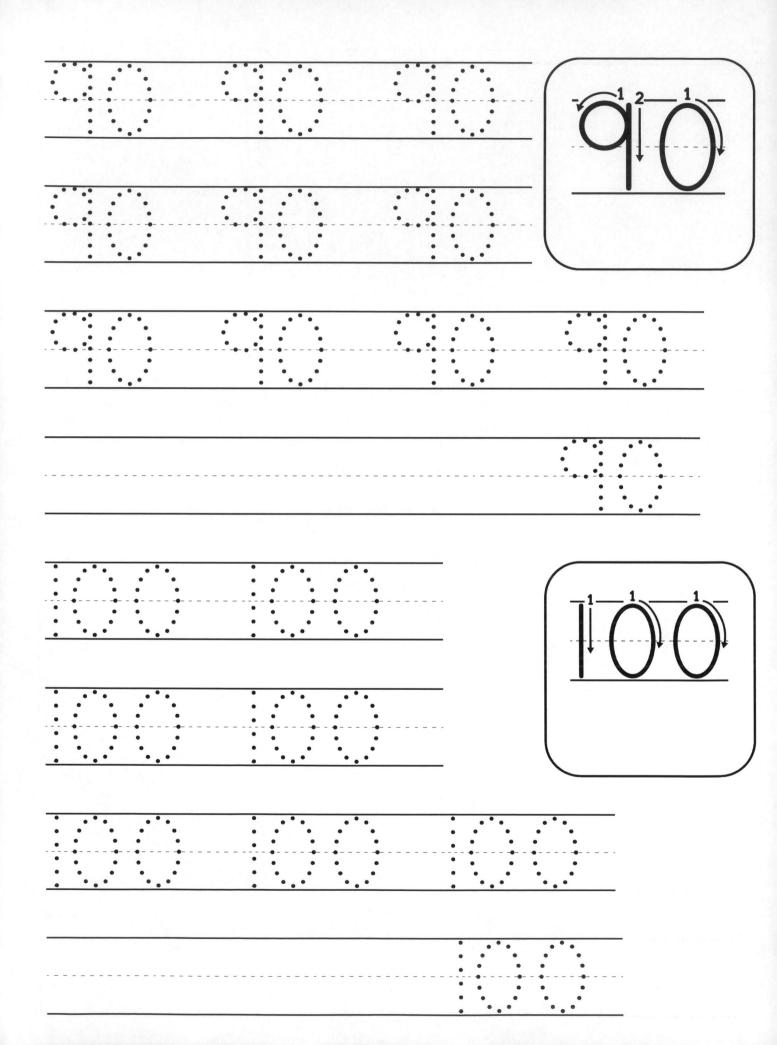

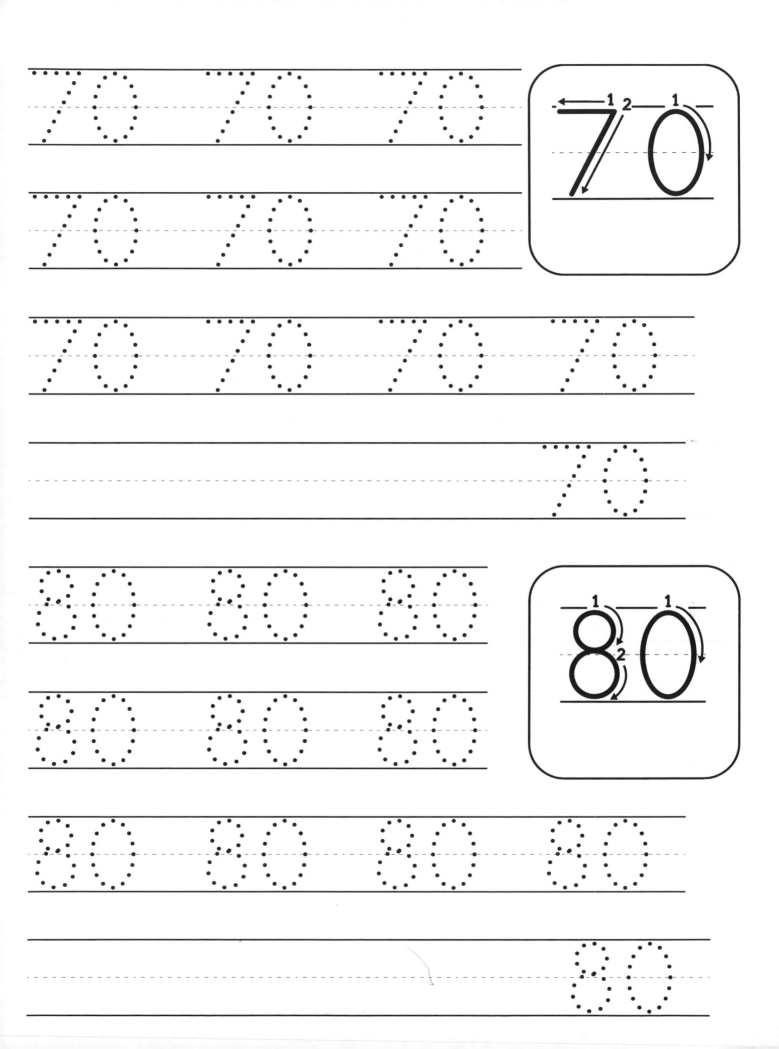

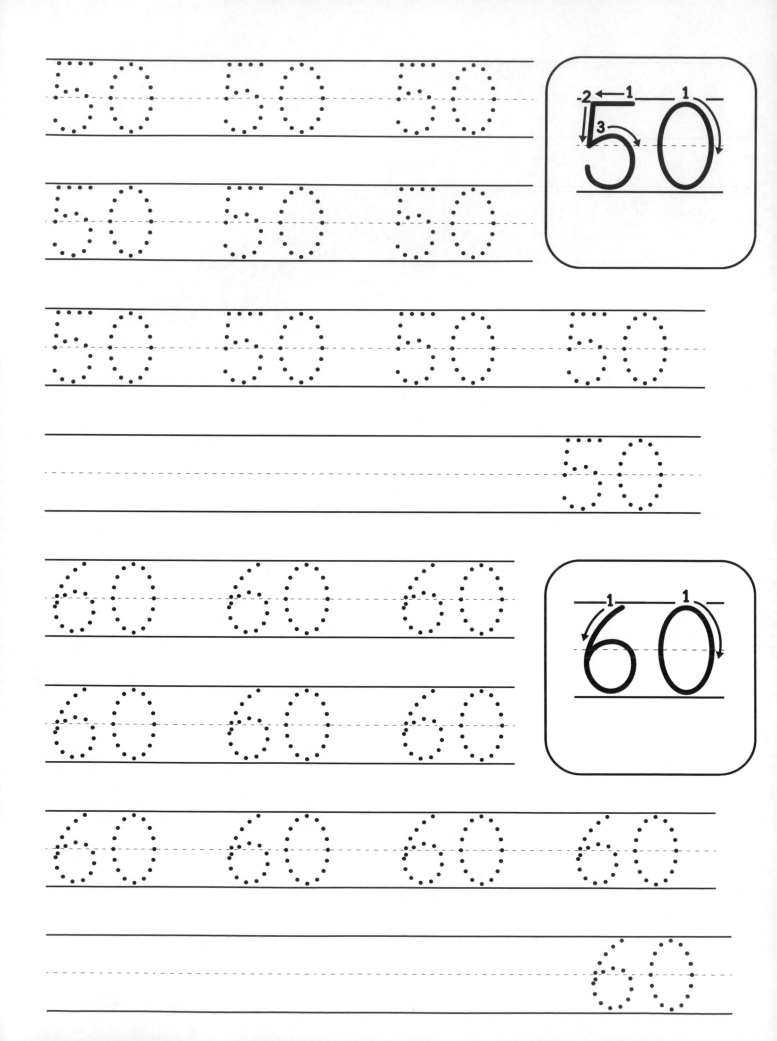

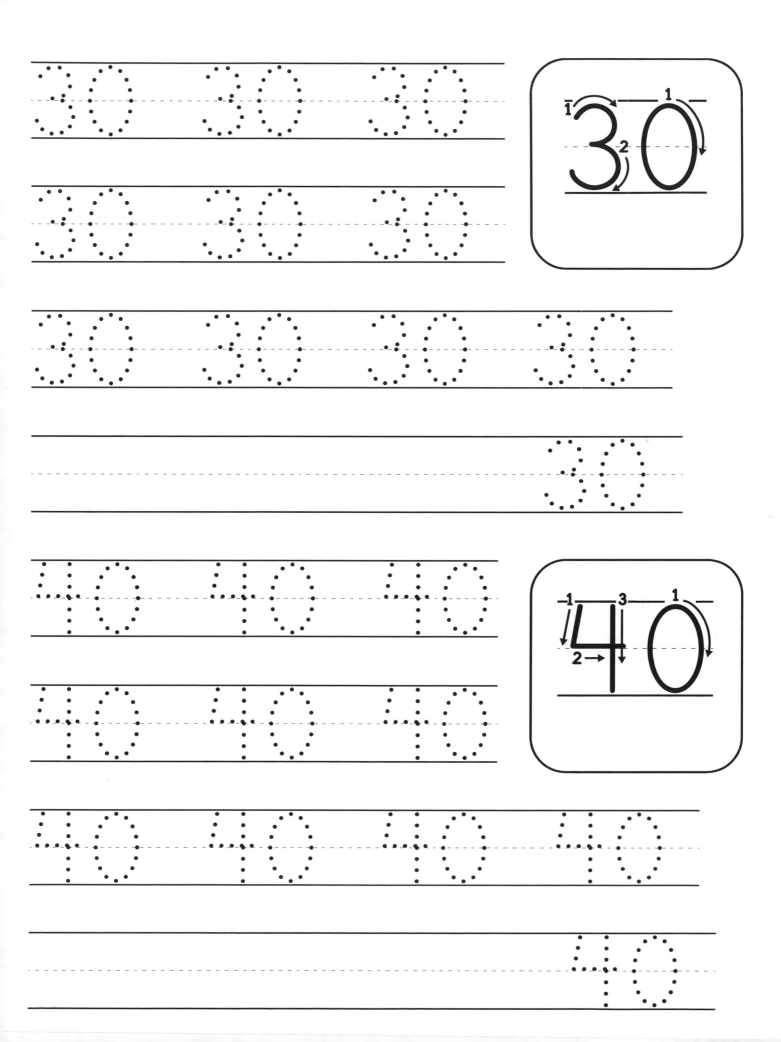

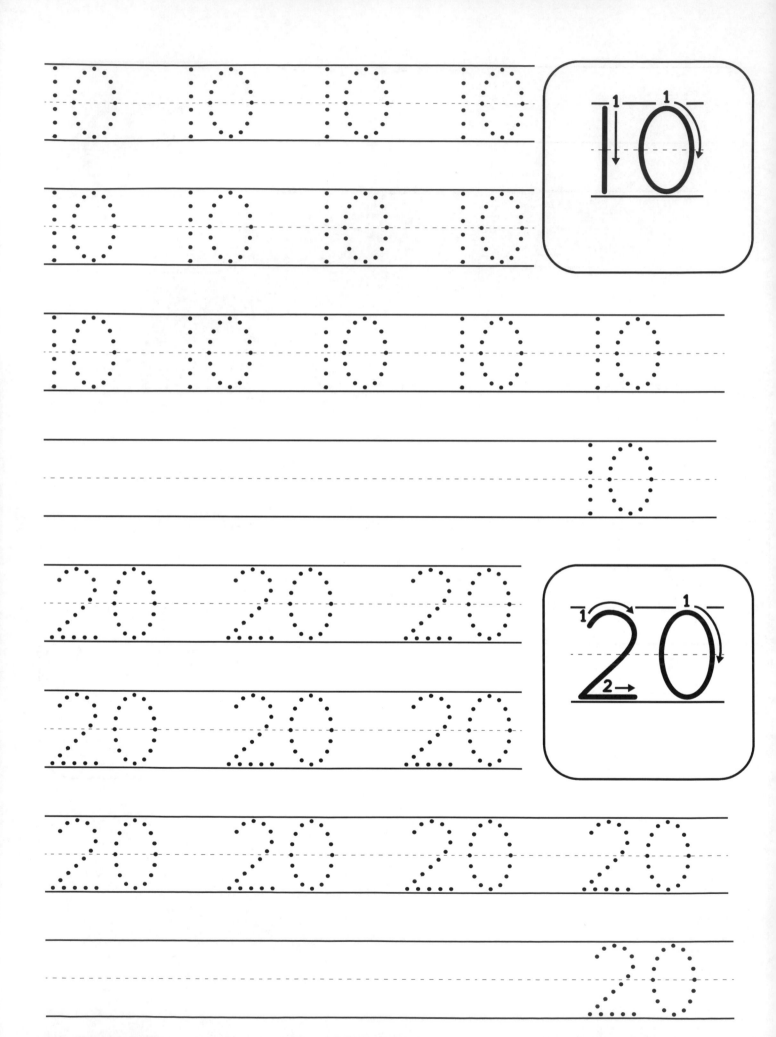

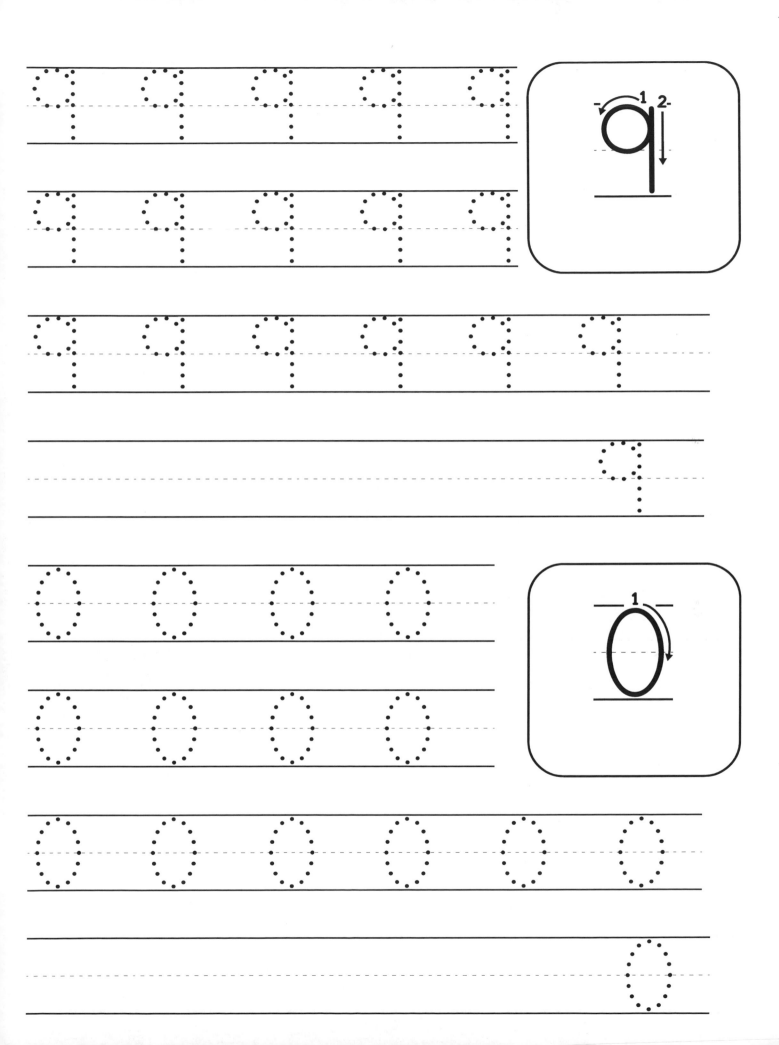

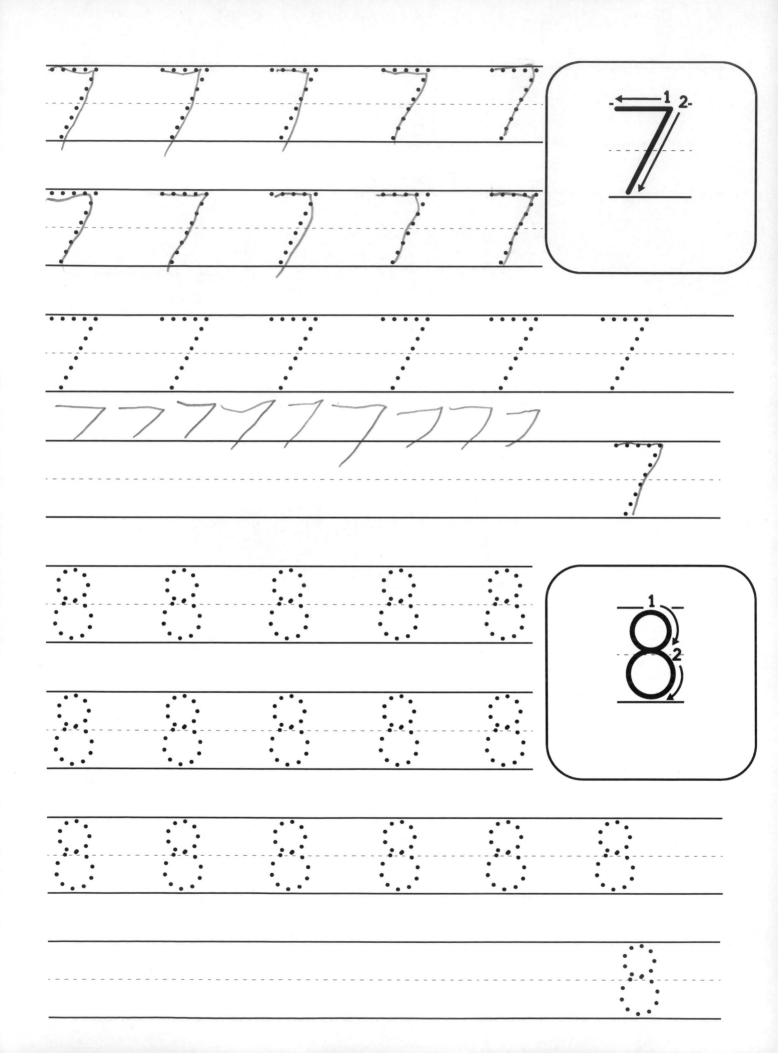

5 5 5 5 5

5 5 5 5 5

5 5 5 5 5 5

5

6 6 6 6 6

6 6 6 6 6

6 6 6 6 6 6

6

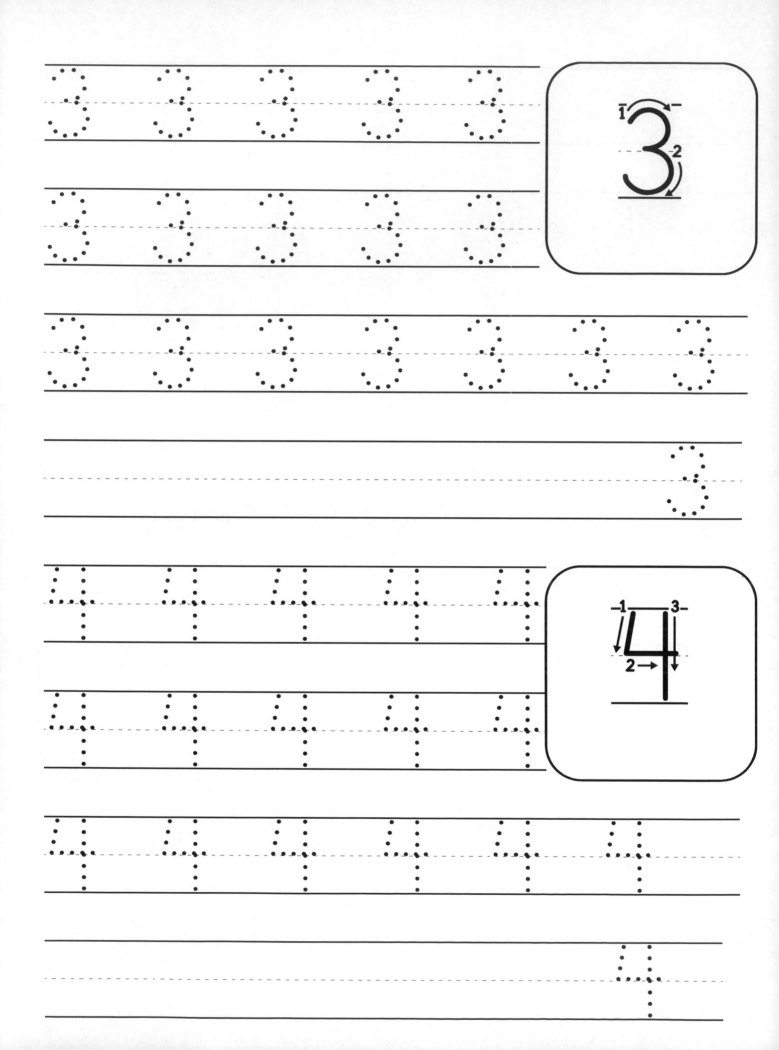

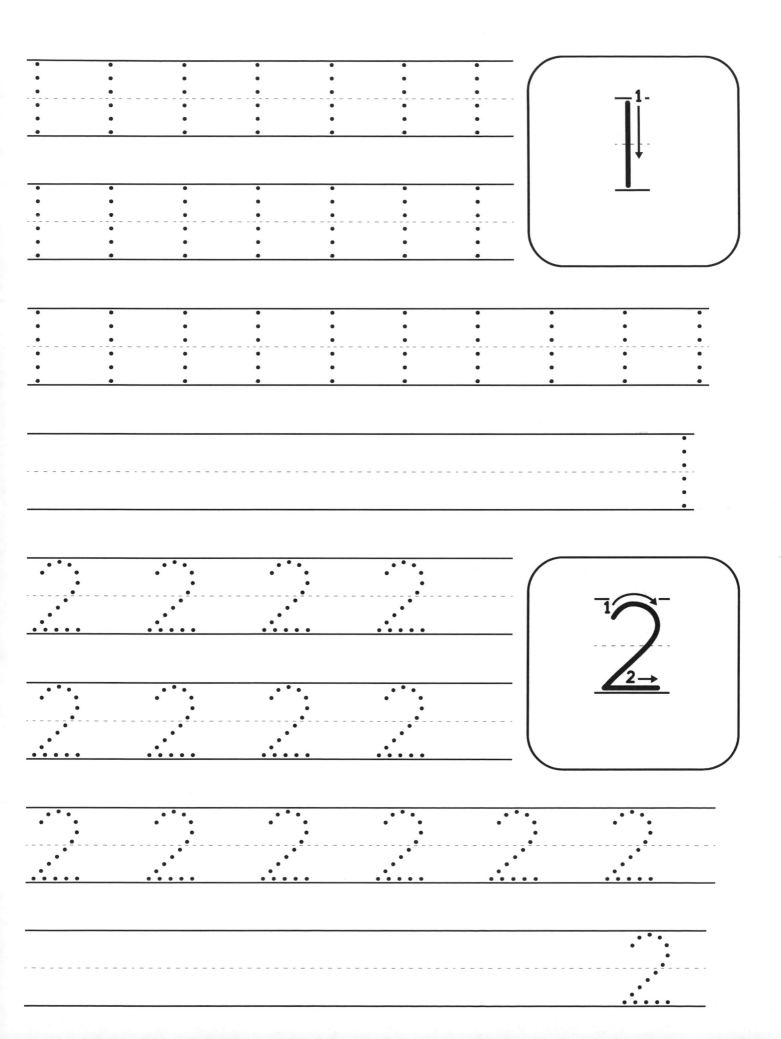

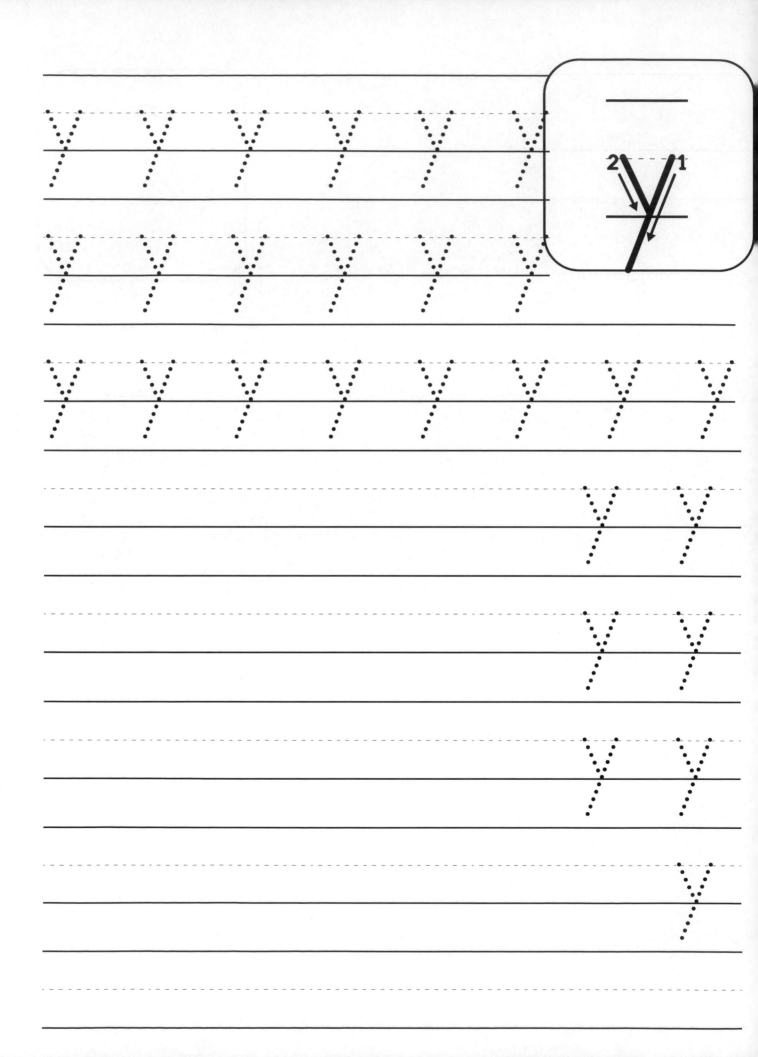

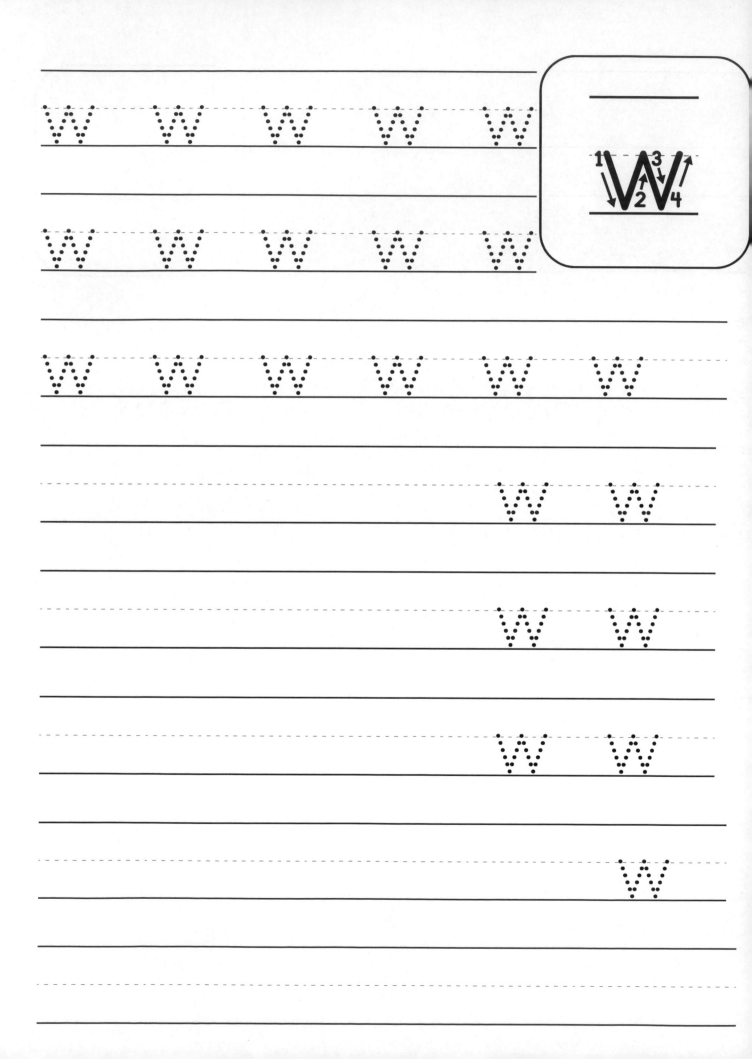

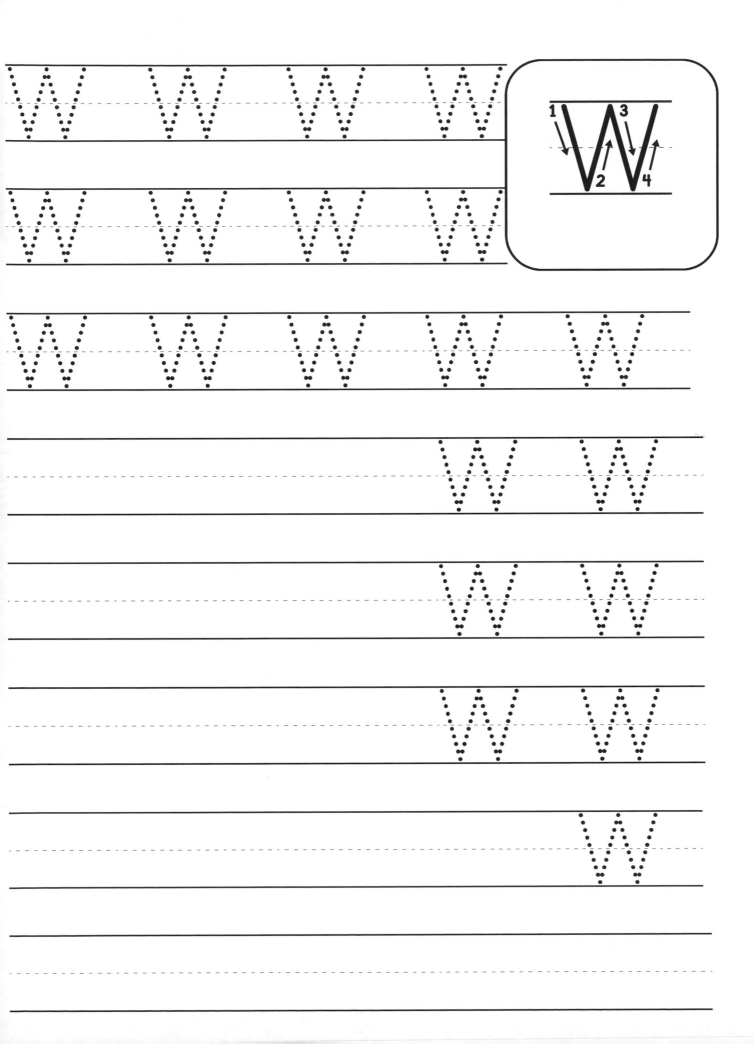

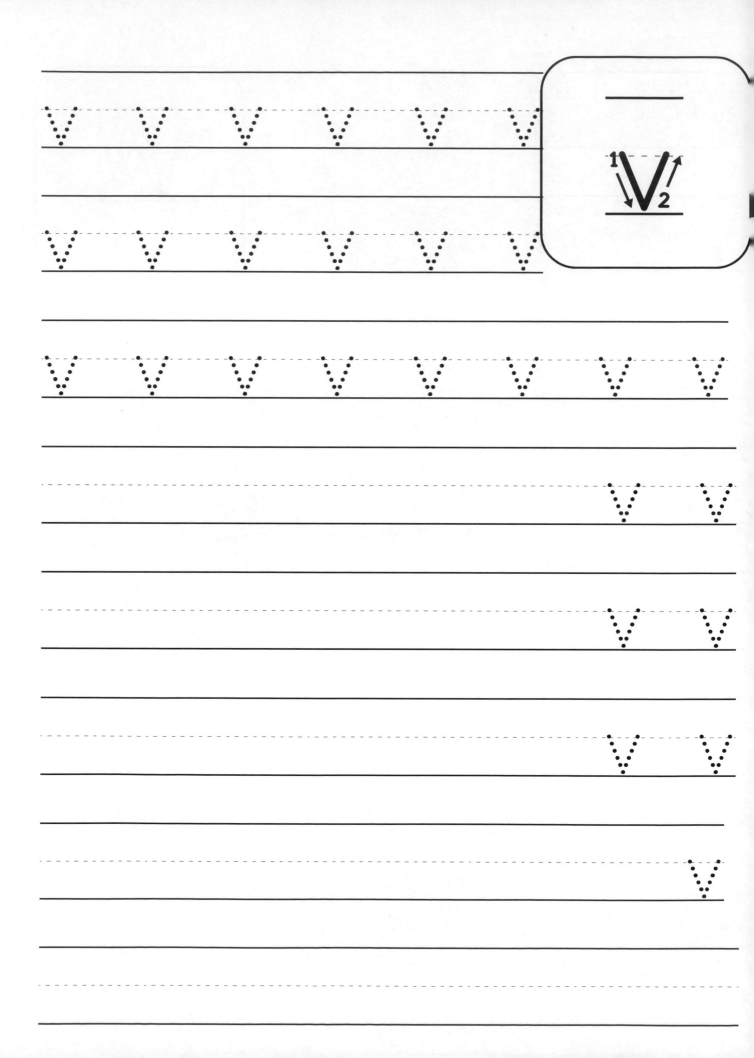

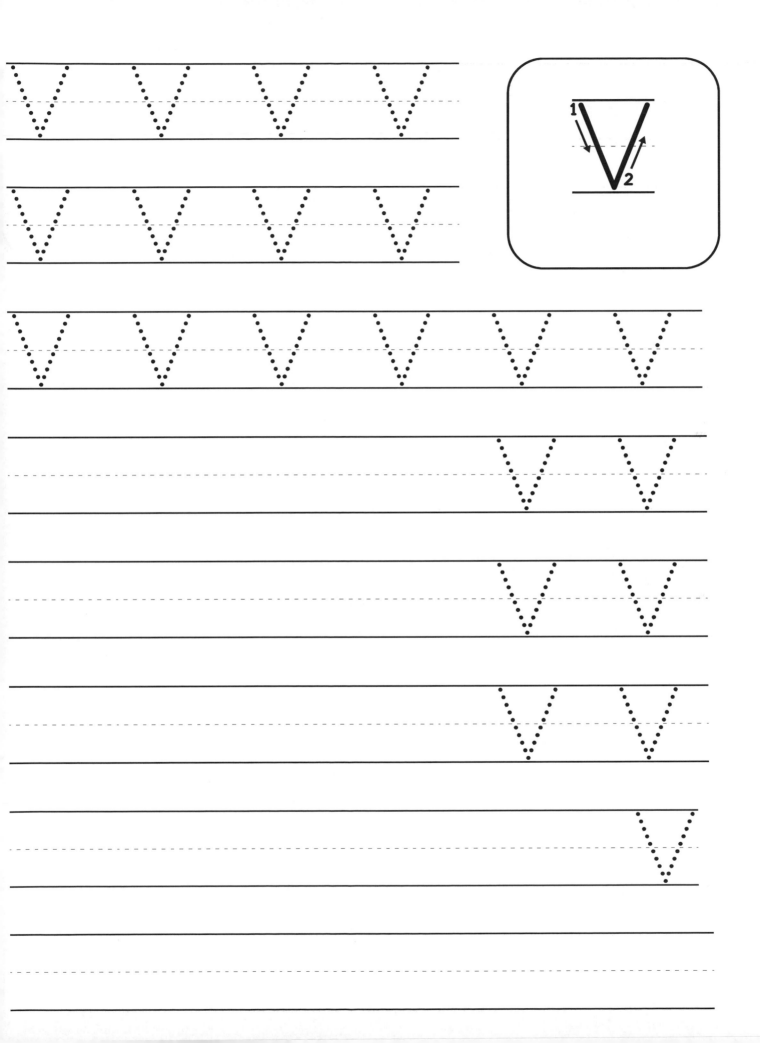

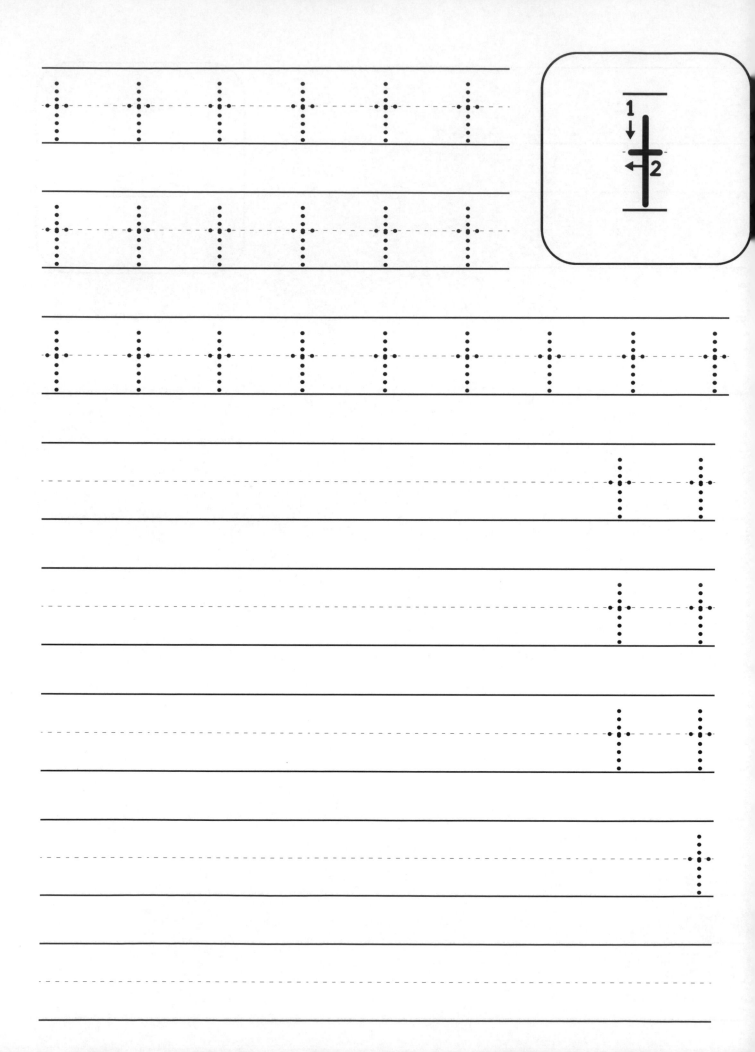

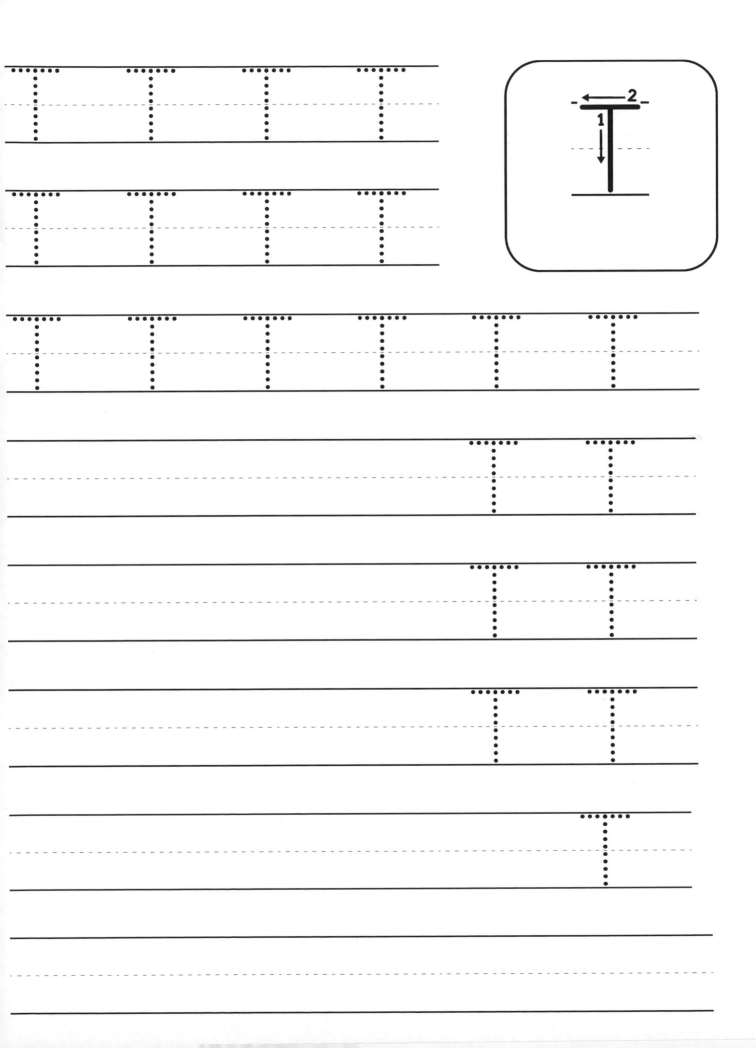

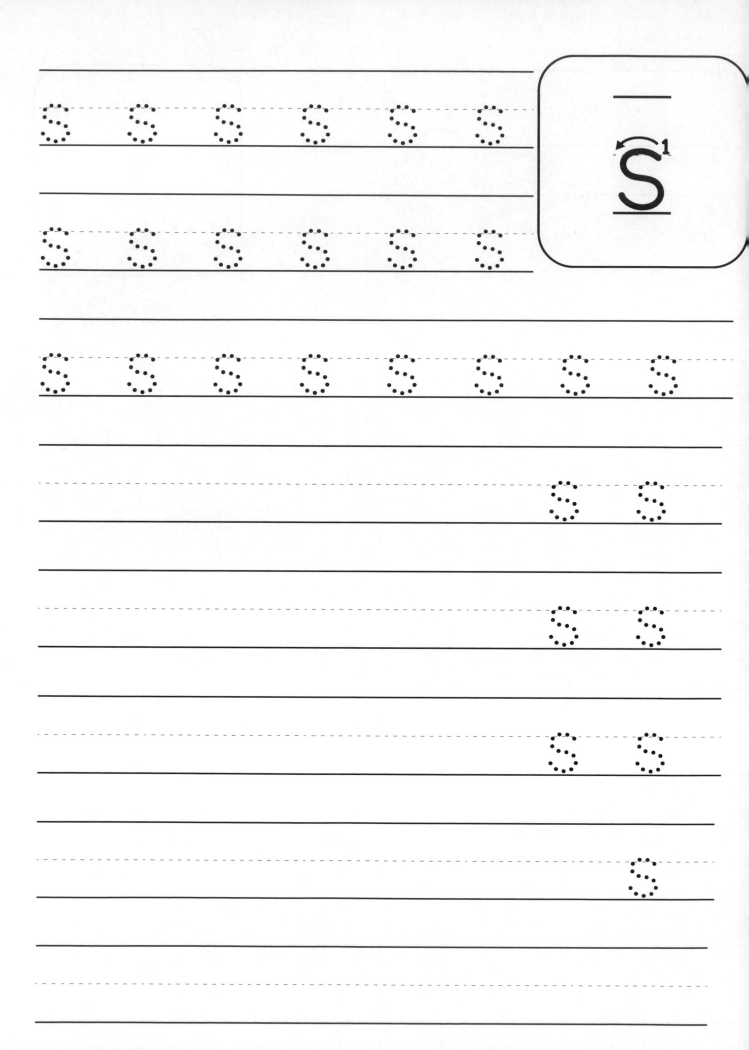

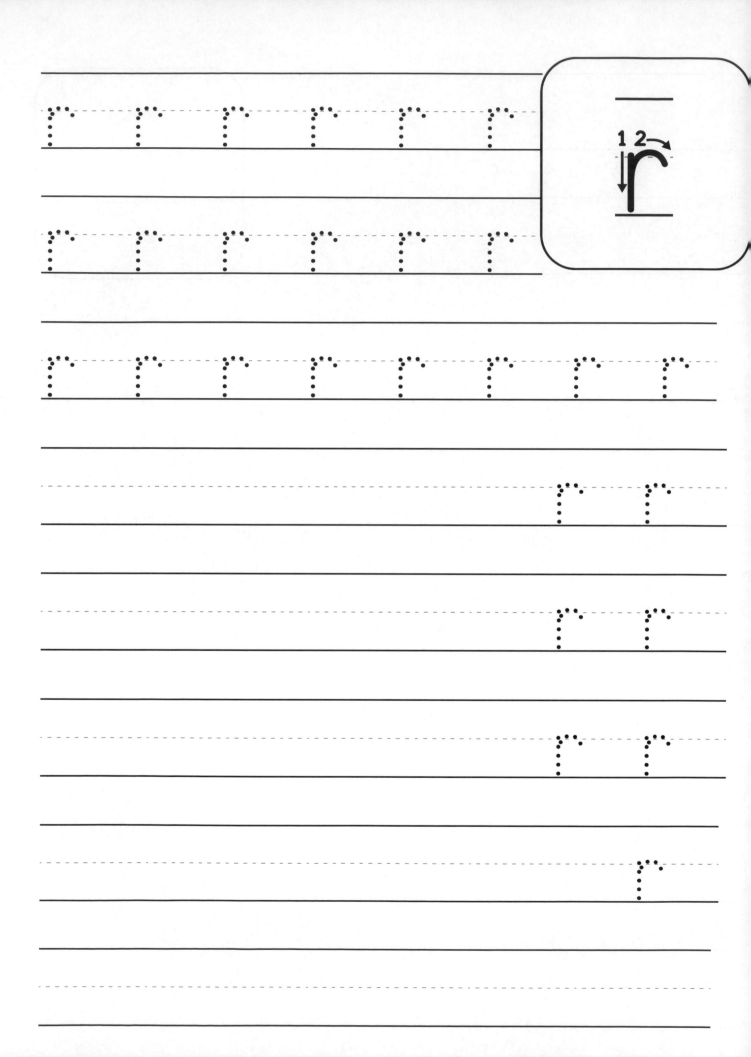

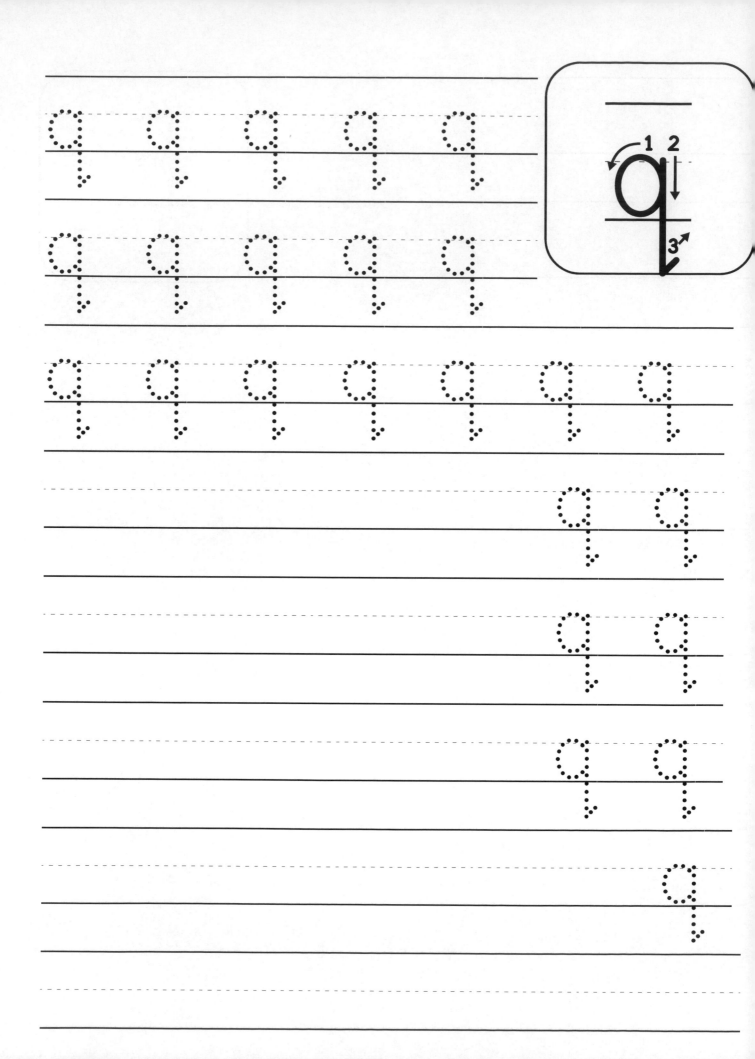

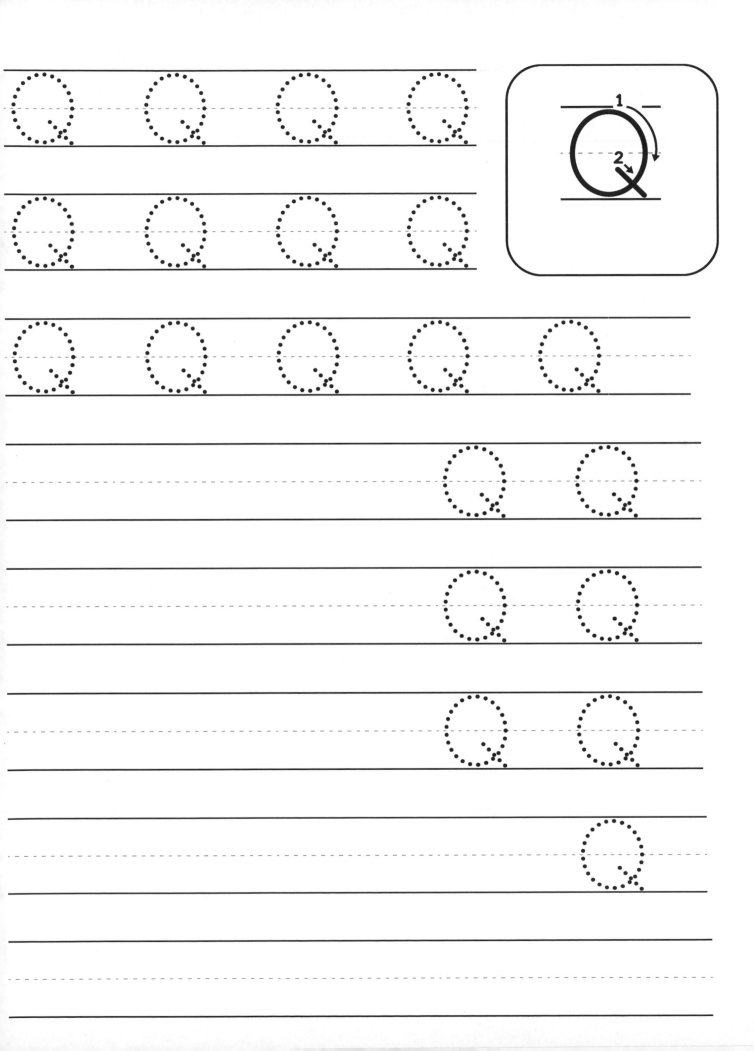

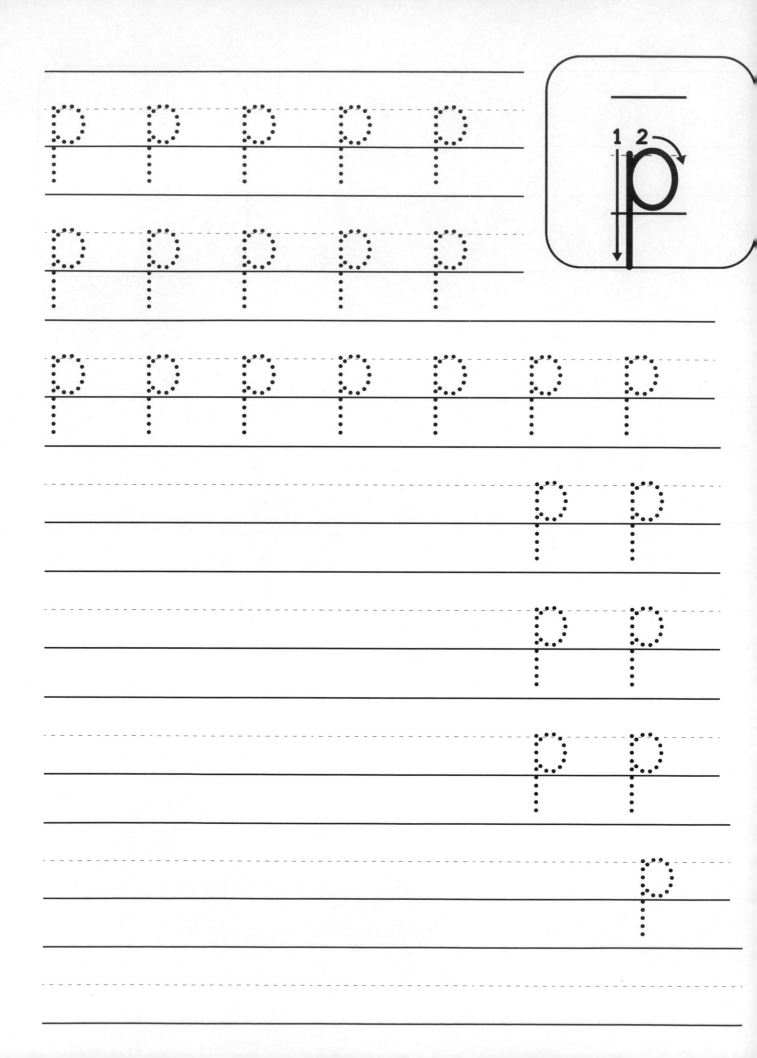

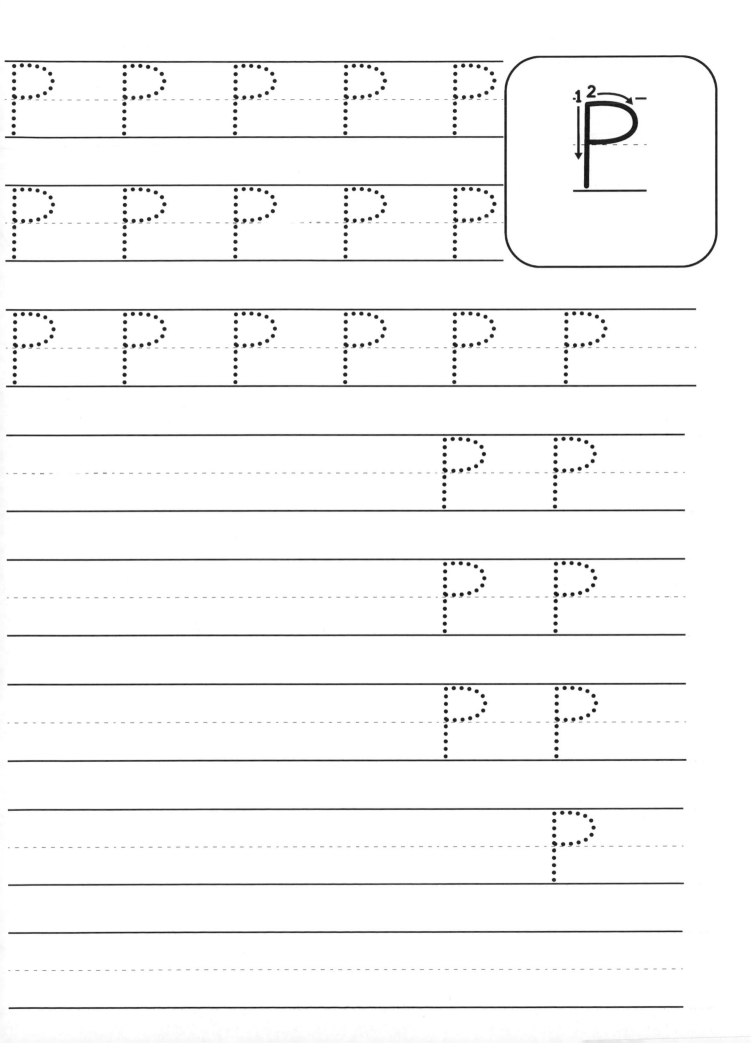

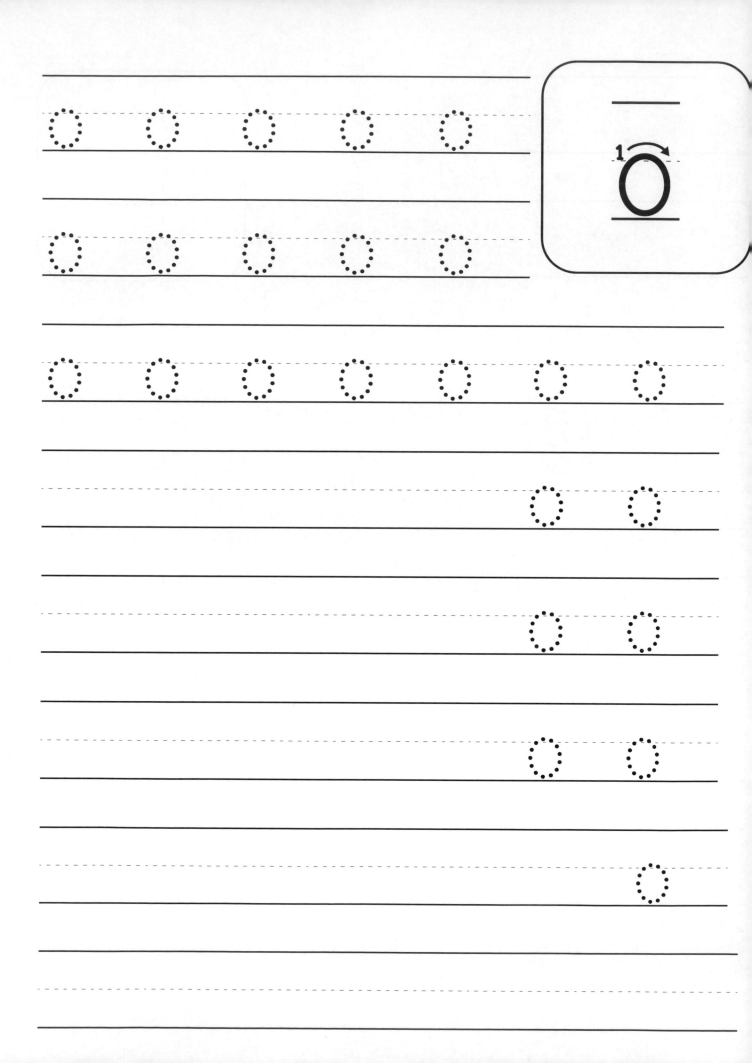

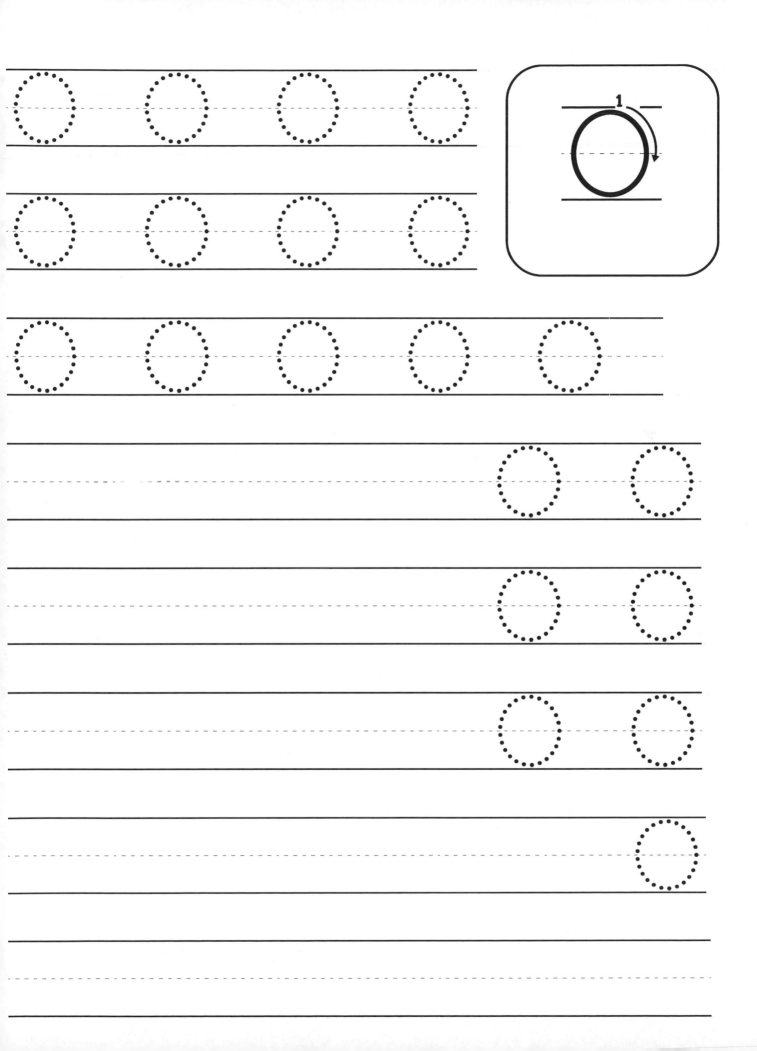

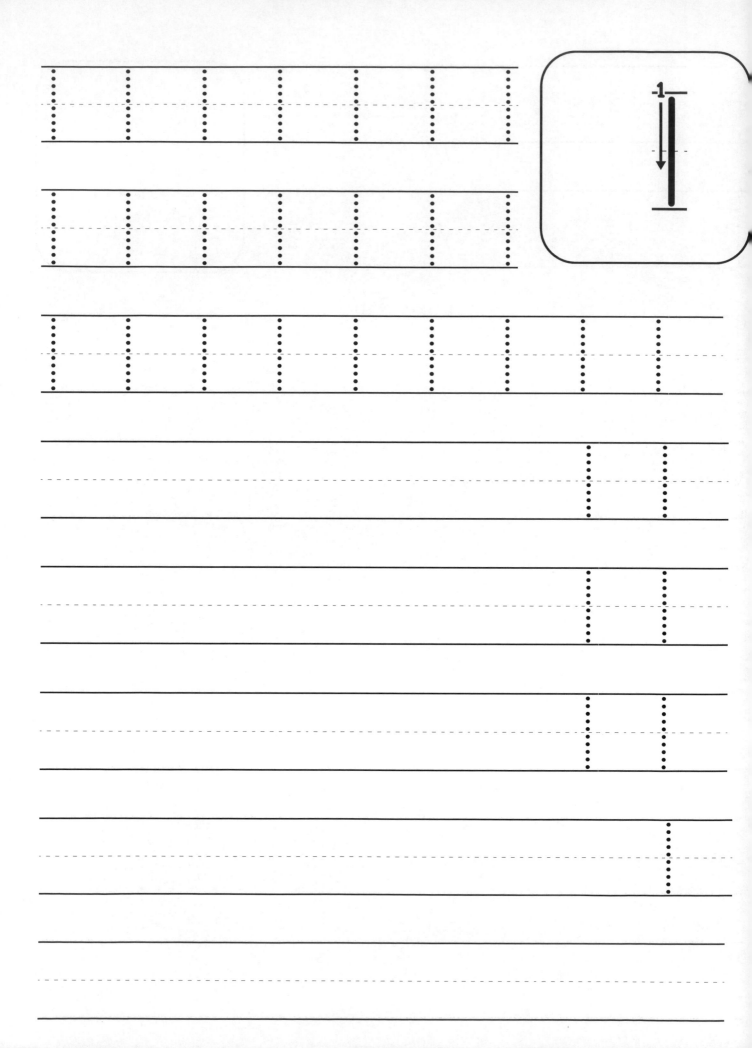

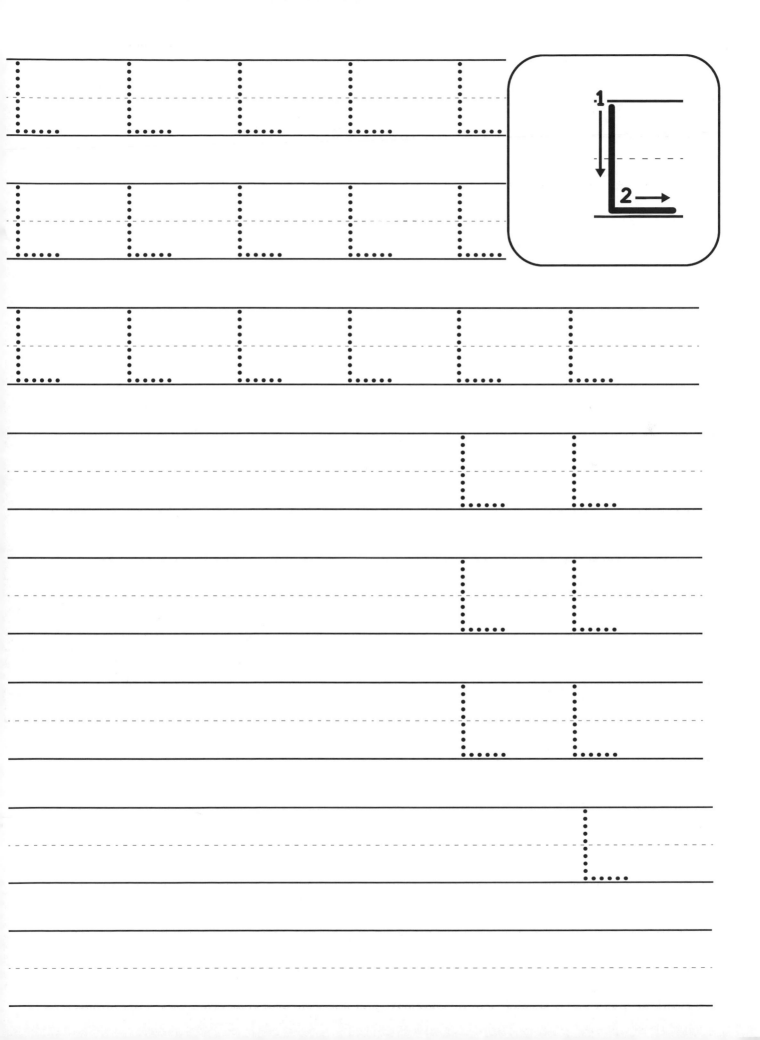

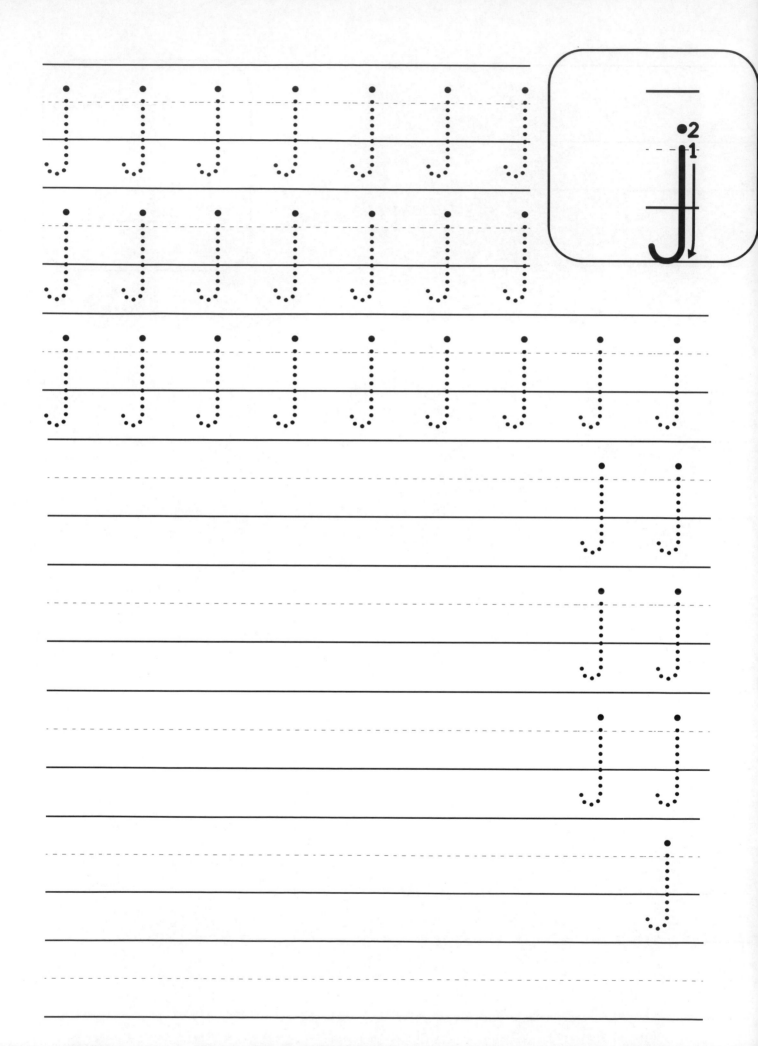

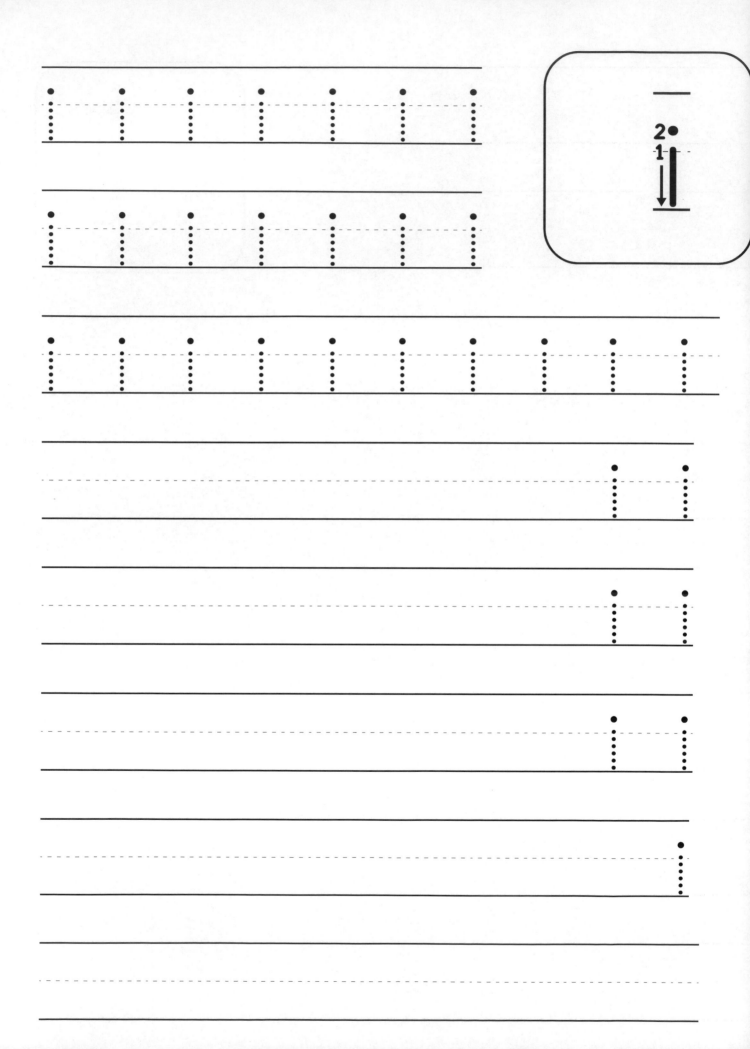

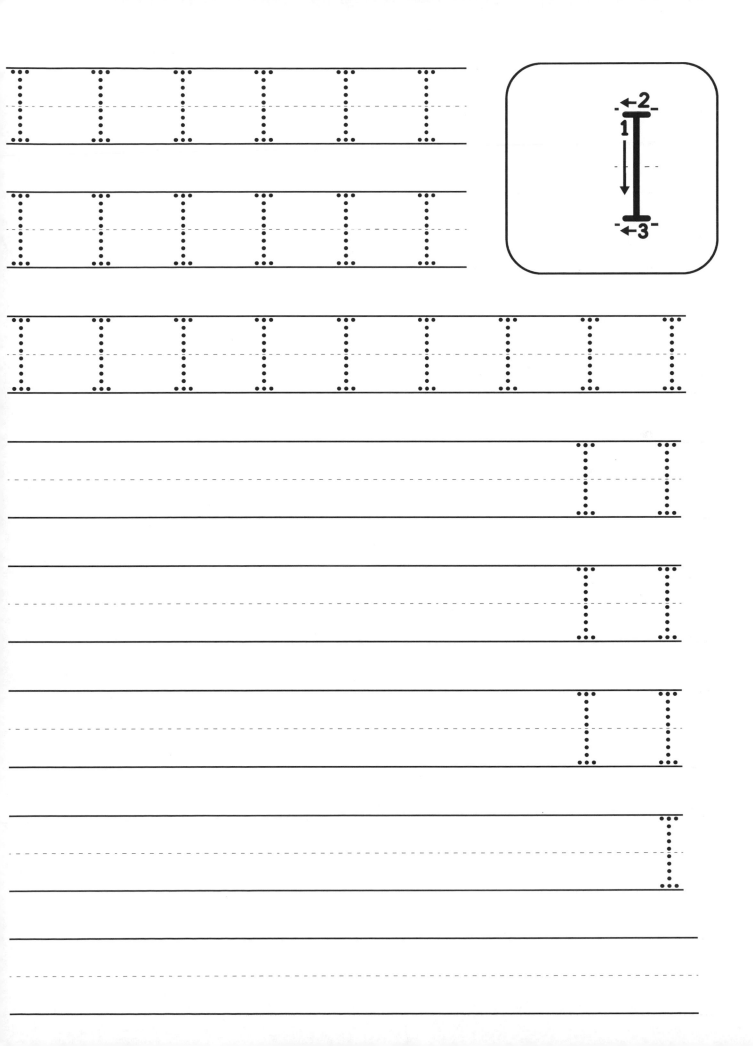

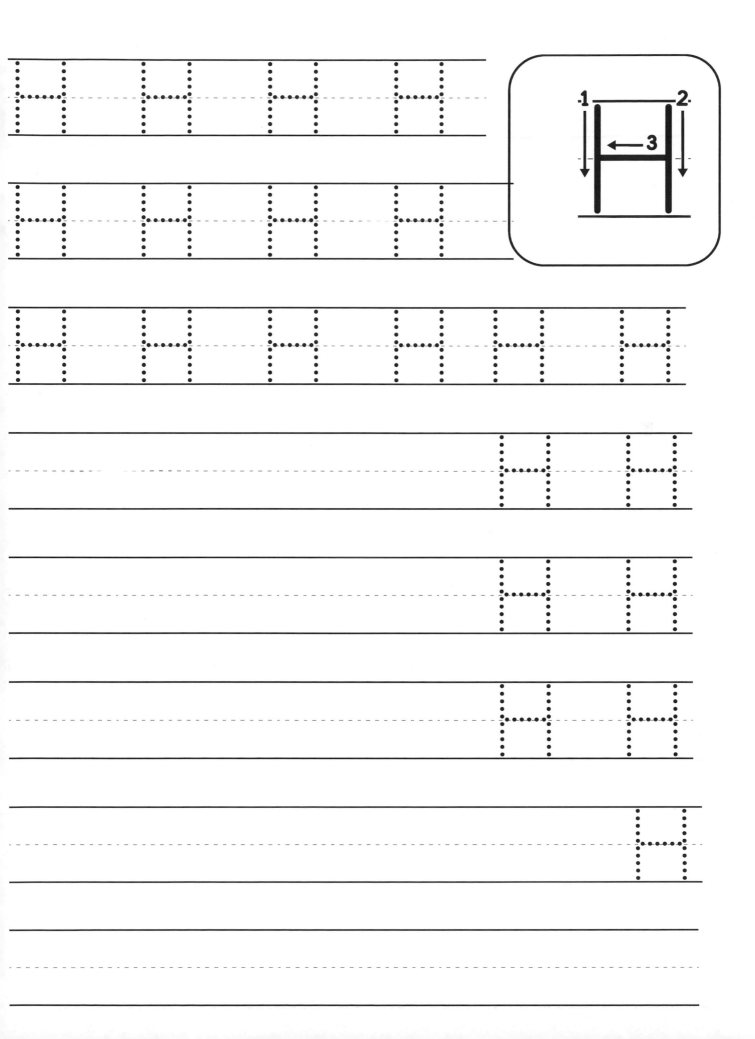

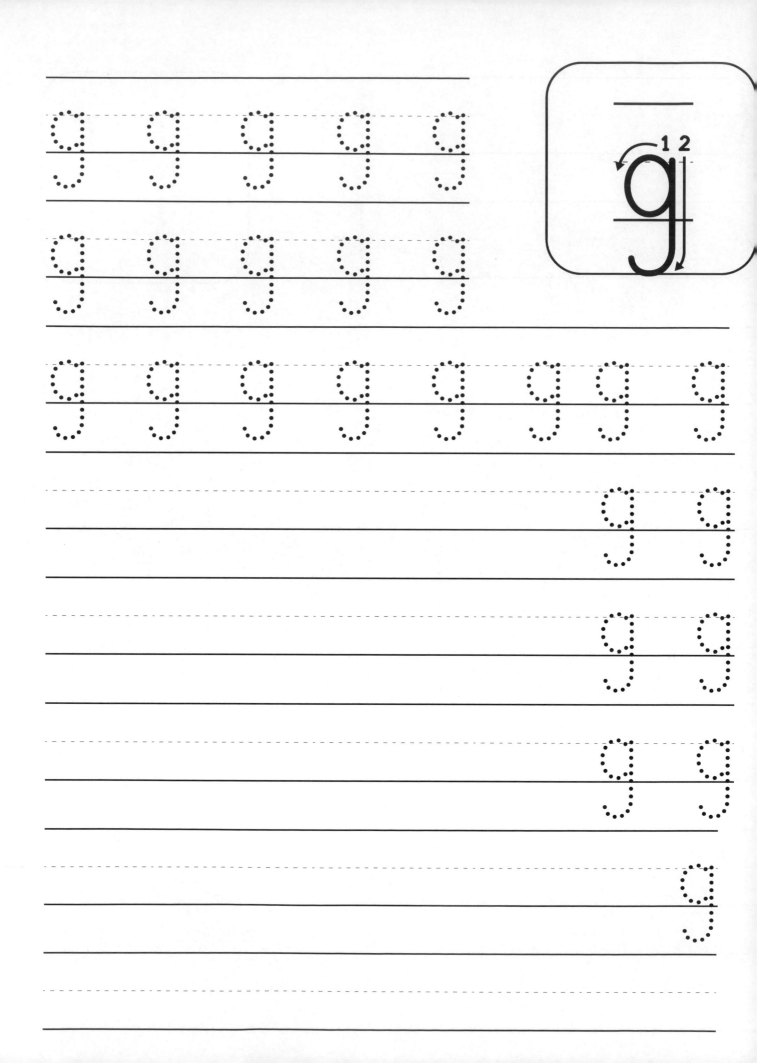

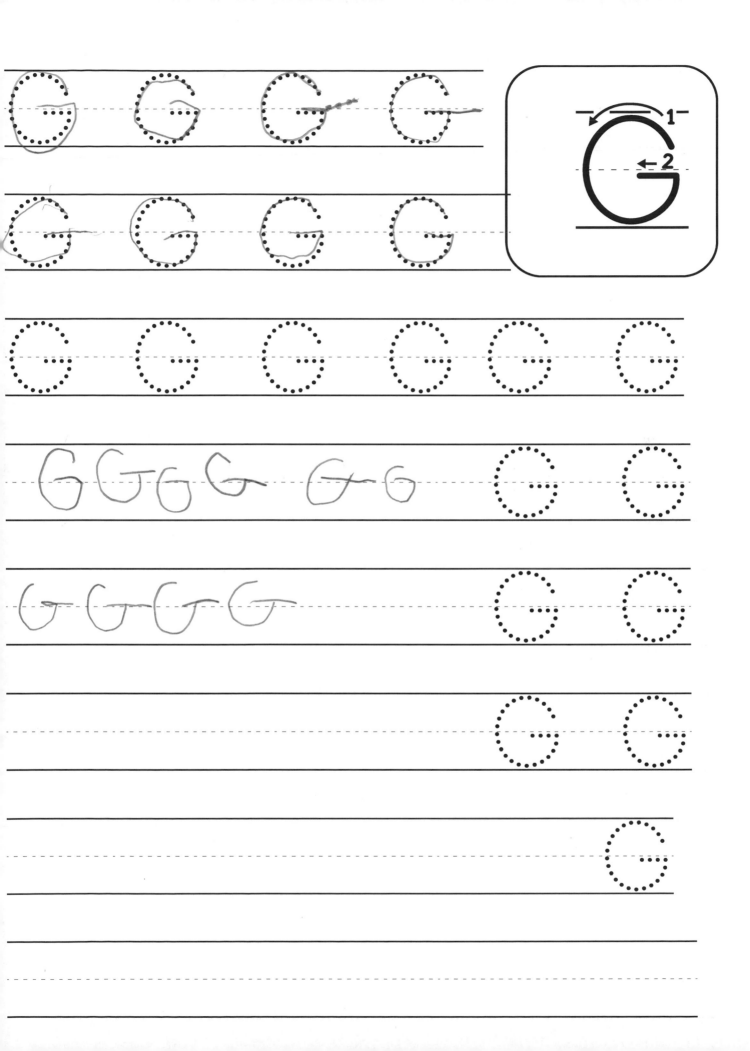

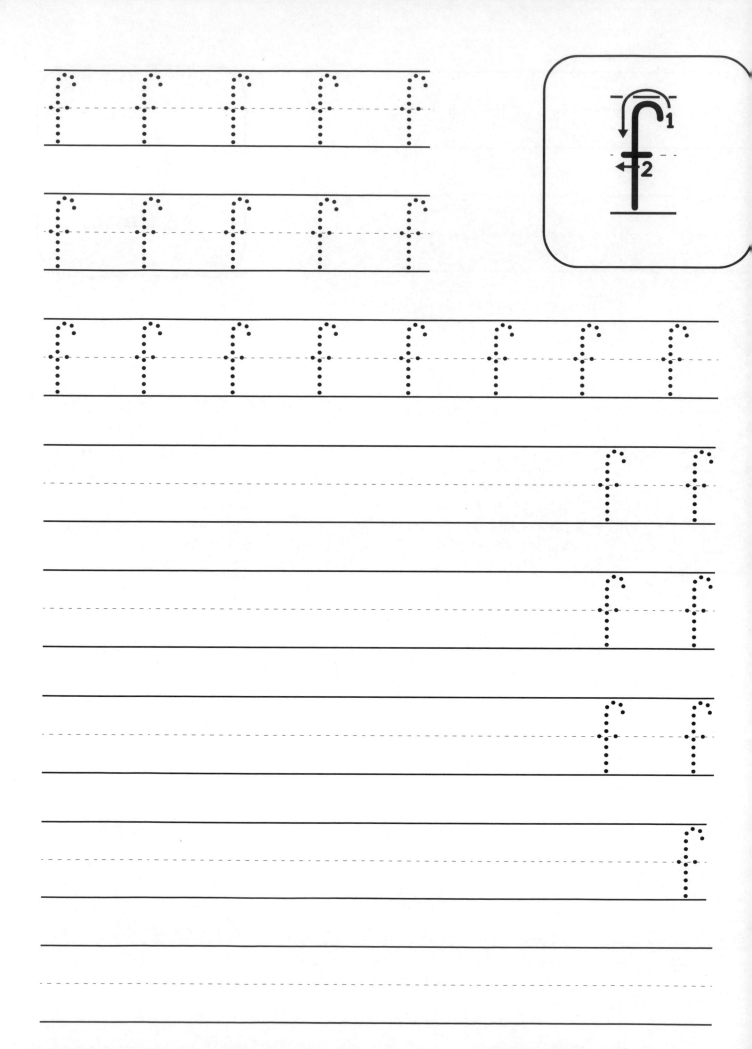

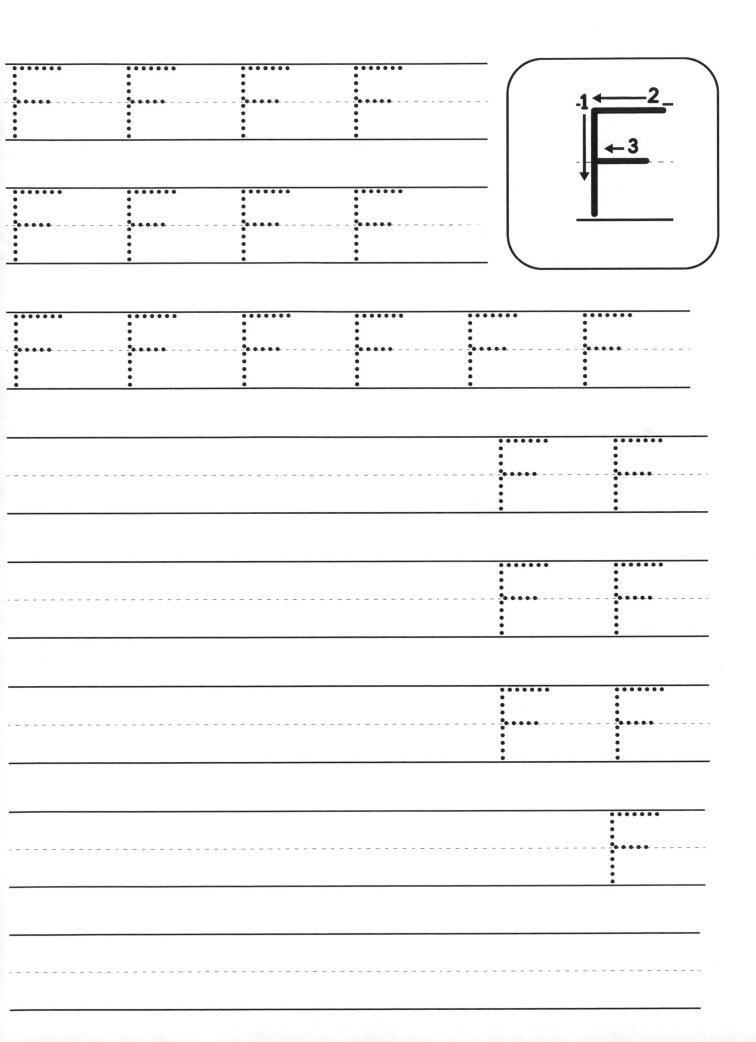

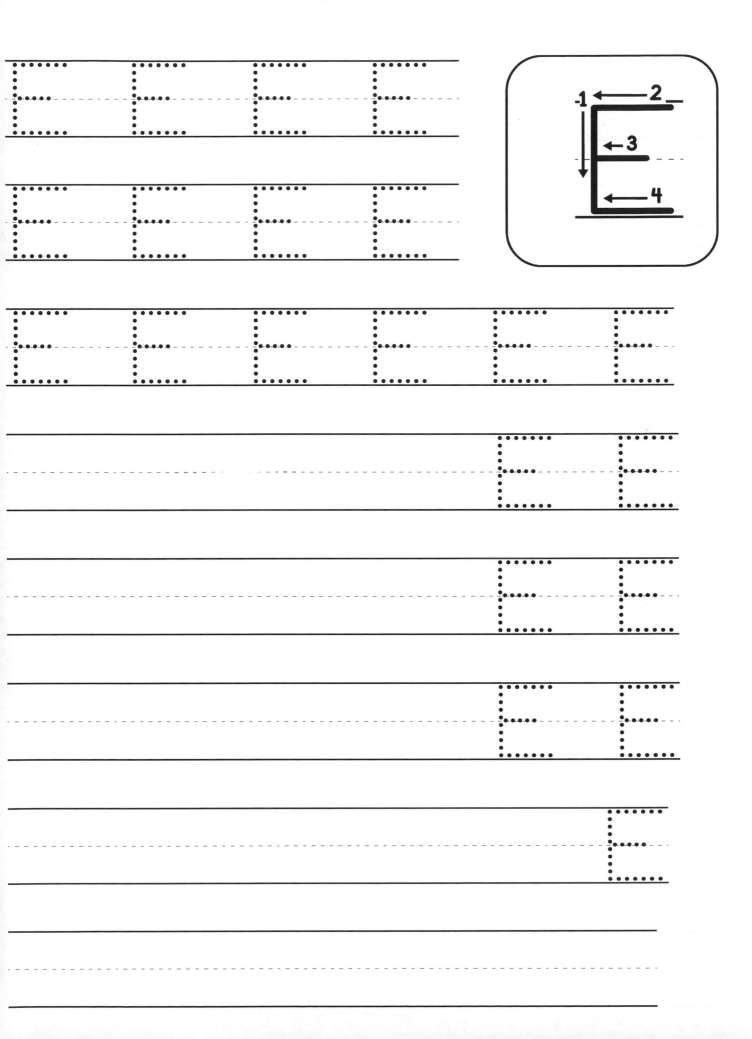

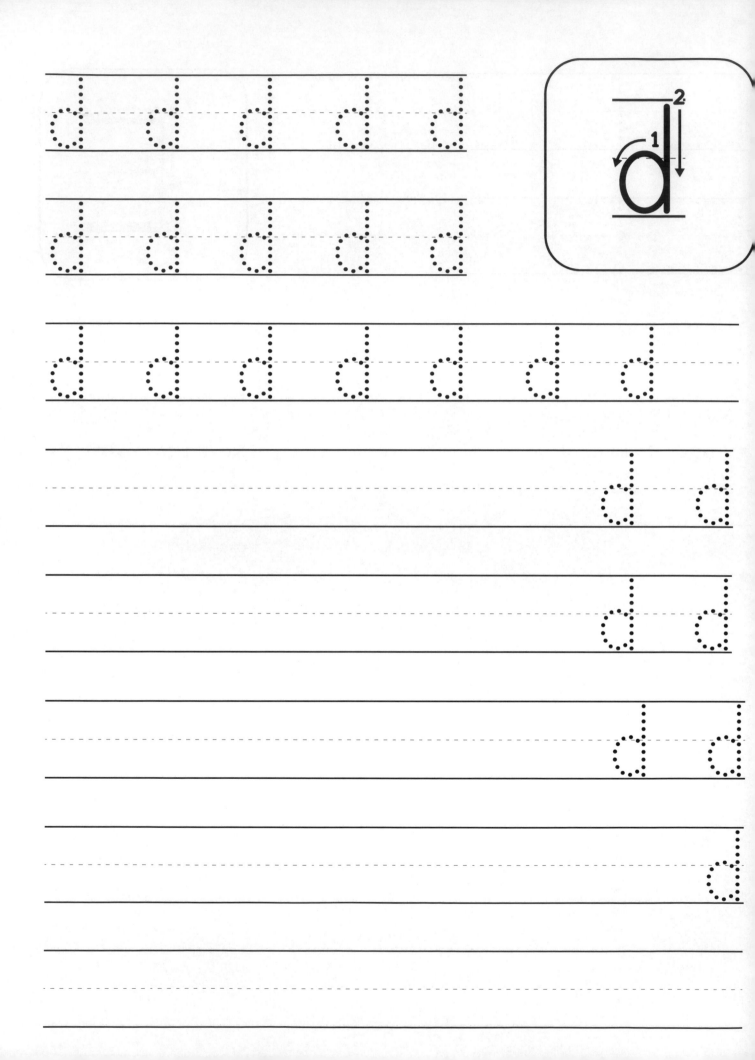

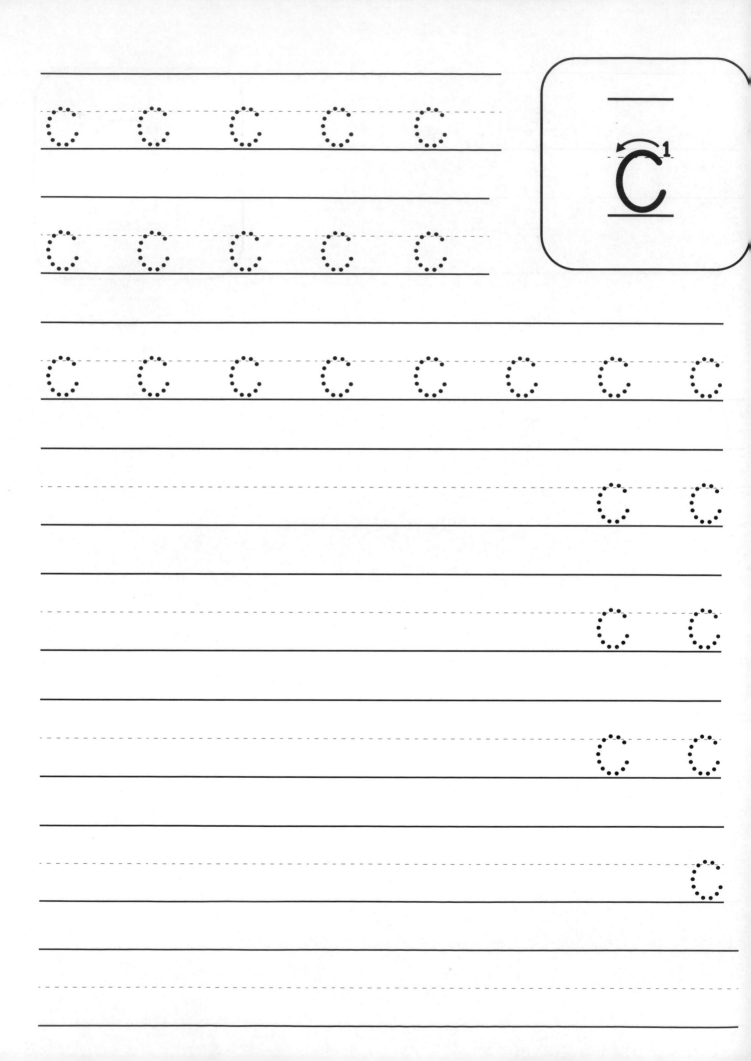

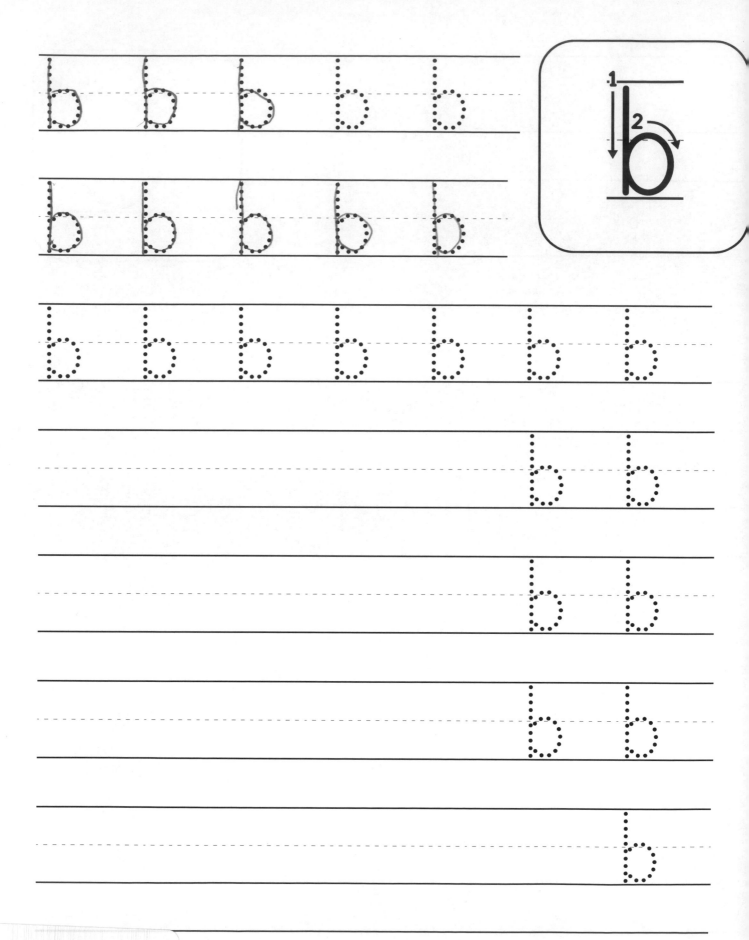